Basic e-Book Creation and Publishing

JACOB SIMON ONOJA AUDU

ISBN:

ISBN-13:

DEDICATION

This Book is dedicated to God almighty for giving me Dr David Agbaje as a leader and friend.

CONTENTS

ACKNOWLEDGMENTS

I thank Dr David Agbaje for introducing me to eBook Publishing and new knowledge.

CHAPTER ONE

Introduction

e-book Publishing is the modern way of delivering literary works and other content, without the rigours of writing and doing all the vast number of things from book idea, book manuscripts, chapter arrangement, book formatting, editing and al the gamut of activities, to bring a book literally from nothing unto the shelf in a bookshop.

In this book, we intend to cover the history of writing and printing and publishing, and the various developments that led to the modern digital printing revolution in 1991, and how amazon has taken advantage of this technology to help budding authors concentrate on their may work, writing, and publish without much ado, for a global audience. This increases the reach and market. So also the fame and fortune, if the book is really good. it helps talents to shine.

CHAPTER TWO

Printing and Publishing: From Johannes Gothenburg to Jeff Bezos

Printing is the art of impressing words or picture or motifs on media, be it clay, stone, pottery, papyrus, cloth paper, wax animal skin or any other media to display them or convey ideas and concepts. It is a form of writing, mechanically aside from scribes manually using pens or other writing materials to put ideas on various media as canvas.

The modern printing press was invented by Johannes Gothenburg a German gold smith in 1440. Gothenburg started his work at Strasburg in France but later moved to his native Germany, where he perfected the printing press.

Before this, all writings were on wax and parchment. Scribes needed special skills to write on scrolls. About 350 BC the Proto Elamite and Sumerian civilizations usually certified documents written on clay. Other forms of printing include

1. block seals,
2. hermant coinage
3. pottery imprint
4. cloth printing

By the year 200 AD the Chinese had developed a method of printing impressions on cloth.

This no doubt included writings on cloth and wood blocks. These were replaced and transferred to paper by 7th century AD. This led to book production in Asia and small-scale publishing, therefrom. This invention involved coating of wooden blocks with ink and pressing them unto paper, for leaving the impression. Later the wood blocks were replaced with metal

In1440. Johannes Gothenburg, invented the modern press in Strasburg France. He later moved to his native country Germany.

By 1450, he had a printing press perfected and ready for commercial large-scale printing. He replaced the wooden blocks with metal blocks and used then to form sentences and pressing them unto paper. He infused ink on the metal blocks making sheets of paper run and roll over the blocks on a cylindrical drum or roller. That was the beginning of mechanized printing and large scale and quicker and more quality assured printing, removing manual errors. The printing machine evolved from the Gothenburg press in 1450 to the rotary press in 1843 to the off-set press in 1875. This used solid ink as the slod ink press. The off-set press further evolved from off-setting to direct digital imaging uno the paper, or direct image printing press or laser press. These use laser to print directly on paper without the need to transfer the images as before. The images are sent directly to the paper on cylinders. This was invented in

1991. With these revolutions in large-scale ability to churn out books and other printing materials, the publishing industry was born with the coming of the commercial printing press and printers. The most recent development of the digital printing era is the online publishing of material as e-Books and paperbacks by Amazon. eBooks are electronic books in electronic format accessible and downloadable and readable in digital format on digital devices like phones and tablets and computers, desktops and laptops. This has been highly developed by Jeff Bezos, a first-class graduate of Princeton in 1986. According to Wikipedia **Jeffrey Preston Bezos** (/ˈbeɪzoʊs/ *BAY-zohss*;[3] né **Jorgensen**; born January 12, 1964)[4] is an American internet

entrepreneur, industrialist, media proprietor, and

investor. Bezos is the founder and CEO[a] of the

multi-national technology company Amazon. He is

the richest person in the world according

to Bloomberg's Billionaires Index.[1]

Chapter Three

Publishing

Publishing is the series of activities that help to covert manuscripts into books in any format. It is the process of creating, developing formatting editing, nd making available in eBook (electronic digital access) or printed on physical paper as a paper back, which is cheaper to buy, or hard cover back, which is more expensive and selective; any content, literary, scientific, periodic, newspapers ie dailies, or directories of manuals or guidebooks or other original or licensed works for public access of making known and available any to the general public any literary or other content, for their reading and use, access. Thus, a publication or a published work even a one page article in a magazine or tabloid or dailies or a much more voluminous work as a full-fledged book, brings the writer and the reader together, so that those writers can transmit their ideas and information to members of the public, usually at a cost. Thus, we may define publishing as the mechanism whereby readers and writers are brought together through the published text or work without physical contact. As a market brings buyers and sellers together in a forum, online or physical, so does a publication or published work bring the writer and the reader to meet mentally, through the work. But some publications are not for a wider audience and as such may be limited in their target audience, like family members, neighbourhood or club or society information, church of social society publications, exclusive to such organizations, as bulletins or other in-house materials or constitutions or guideline, rules and regulations.

But own main concern here are books and other materials for the general public and audience even the global village. This is large-scale publishing.

Publishing can also be

a) commercial

b) Self-publishing or

c) Hybrid.

We can also have the publishing of

Dailies like Newspapers and bulletins especially trade and market and weather reports.

Periodicals like magazines and tabloids

We can have formal books

And directories as reference materials, Census repots and annual reports of companies and charities and other non-profit and for-profit organizations.

Movie and Tv show scripts

CHAPTER FOUR

The Standard Format For A Book

In publishing books over the years, a certain discernible format and internationally recognized format and standardization of books has emerged.

A Book is expected to have the following format:

1. The Title or front cover page and back Cover page.

2. The copyright

3. Dedication

4. Acknowledgements

5. Forward

6. Preface

7. Table of content

8. Introduction

9. The main body of the work, the real content, which

    could be many chapters.

10. Blurb: executive summary of the work

11. About the Author

Chapter Five

Short Notes on The Various Items in The Book

1. The Cover or Title page

This is the front cover of the Book and it is the

front outside of the book. It contains the title, of

the book. Book titles assist shelf readers and

people to search for an get the exact content they

seek. This title is also generally and usually printed

at the height-back of the Book so that if it it

stacked standing in a library, we can see the title

not from the front or back but from the ridge of the

Book. The ridge is the part between the front cover

and the back cover of a book which is equivalent

to its height, if you look at the book as a solid with three dimensions.

Thus, the title of the book should as much as possible reflect the content of the book. It should indicate the subject area and the issued dealt there as much as possible and practicable. A book should normally be judged by its title. You cannot title a book *Basic Economics* and start to present items of cookery or drama within or Home economics. This is inappropriate and very misleading and will even be rejected by any serious publisher. It could have adverse effects on the books sales.

2. THE COPYRIGHT PAGE

All original works, be they literary or artistic or musical compositions or songs or poems or inventions need a copyright. According to Copyright Definition - Investopedia

> https://www.investopedia.com/terms/c/copyright.asp **Copyright** refers to the legal right of the owner of intellectual property. In simpler terms, **copyright is** the right to copy. This means that the original creators of .

A copyright is the right of an author or producer or publisher or anyone so authorised to require anyone who wishes to use the material to get a written permission from the copyright holder. Some publishers require the author to vet this right with the while others retain the right with the author or even hold the right jointly. This information must be clearly indicated. This page contains the International Standard Book Number (ISBN) . it is a unique number of thirteen 13 digits that singularly identifies your book, even amongst books with similar titles or subjects. It helps also to differentiate between the different editions of a book. when a book is revised significantly due to perceived or discovered errors or new knowledge or discoveries, it takes on a new ISBN with the same old title, and may be the edition number. So the first edition of any book carries the number One (1). We can also differentiate between ISBN and ISSN. The International Standard Serial Number, ISSN is used for periodicals and academic or religious or professional journals or the like with Volumes and serial numbers, to differentiate the same long running journal editions from each published edition over the years or centuries.

3. DEDICATION

A person may wish to dedicate his work to any number of persons or entities that he feels need the dedication. Some people dedicate their works to God Almighty, some to their spouses or children of the memory of a late relative or friend or acquaintances or some other people who have significantly impacted their live. Or which they wish to remember and make their memorial public. This is the use of the dedication page.

4. ACKNOWLEDGEMENTS

Acknowledgement is to give honour and recognition to those it is due for their assistance one way or another in the production of the book.

Such may be moral, physical, financial, technical, advisory etc. These might include teachers, copy writers, encouragers, carers, assistants, superiors who allow us some liberty in time etc.

5. FORWARD

The Forward to a book is usually a written positive affirmation of good work and history of the author and or the work, by someone other than the author who introduces the author as known and why such a person thinks we should listen to the author and read their book. It may contain some unique information about the author as seen by another.

6. PREFACE

A preface (/ˈprɛfəs/) or proem (/ˈproʊɛm/) is an introduction to a book or other literary work written by the work's author. An introductory essay written. From

https://en.wikipedia.org/w/index.php?search=preface+to+a+book&title=Special%3ASearch&go=Go&ns0=1

It gives a brief format of the content and is different from the general introduction, which situates the book in the subject area.

7. TABLE OF CONTENT

A table of content is the table for navigating subjects and

topics within the book. It contains all the items from the Cover or Title page, The copyright page, Dedication, Acknowledgements, the Forward, the Preface, the table of content, the Introduction, the main body of the work, the real content, in several chapters or sub topics, and then the summary as the Blurb; clearly indicating the page or range of pages inside the book where each may be found.

8. INTRODUCTION

This is a background to the work to clear the ground, like a form of the need for the book or some other thing that prompted the writing.

9. THE MAIN BODY

The main body of the work, the real content, this will be the content which the author wants t communicate, starting from the foundation to the climax and then the conclusion, it may be a number of chapters and is the greatest volume of the work usually.

Chapter six

BLURB

This is an executive summary of the content of the book and if there may be any need for a follow up or some other thing. All these come in the Blurb. It is the conclusion of the book. It usually gives the book its takeaway flavour, as the last impression on the reader. It should be brief and concise. It should be about a page at or two at most.

ABOUT THE AUTHOR

Sir Jacob Simon Onoja Audu *ksm*, is a graduate of Geography from the University of Jos Nigeria and holds an MBA International Business Management from the Lagos State University 1981 and 2008 respectively.

He is well-travelled and a self-taught man, who has expanded his knowledge through private reading and seminars and courses online and in the classroom.

He taught briefly at Adeyemi College of Education, Ondo in Ondo state and at the Nigeria Customs College Ikeja as a serving Customs officer.

He joined the Nigeria Customs Service after graduation in and

NYSC in 1982 and rose through the ranks to the rank of Comptroller of Customs, He retired the public service in 2017 and he is into private business, Business Advisory and Tax Consulting.

He is happily married with many children and resides in Lagos, Nigeria. He is a trained and Commissioned catechist in the Catholic Church and has attended many courses and seminars in Christian theology. He is a trained UNCTAD ASYCUDA Program Manager from the West African Computer Institute at Lomé, Togo. He has attended many courses on Customs Valuation, Risk Assessment, Customs Risk Profiling and Investigations.